Bed and Breakfast:

Slum Housing of the Eighties

Jean Conway and Peter Kemp

SHAC

Set up in 1969, SHAC was London's first housing aid centre. It is unique in that it is the only organisation offering help to all client groups throughout London. Its work covers the whole range of housing problems, including homelessness, security of tenure, disrepair and mortgage arrears. To date, SHAC has advised and helped more than 100,000 households.

In addition to its advice work, SHAC undertakes research into the major housing issues of the day, and provides information and training for a wide range of voluntary and statutory organisations.

Cover photo supplied by Camden HMO Group

Printed by Calvert's Press (TU), 55 Mount Pleasant, London WC1X 0AE.
© SHAC, 189a Old Brompton Road, London SW5.
1985

SHAC receives financial support from the Department of the Environment, the Greater London Council, and many other public authorities and private and corporate donors.

Contents

Acknowledgements	4
Introduction	5
The problem	5
Structure of the report	6
1: Why the increase?	7
Cuts in public rented housing	7
The focus on owner occupation	9
The continuing shortage	10
The continuing decline of the private rented sector	11
The inevitable consequence	13
2: The financial cost	14
The numbers increase	14
The cost to central government	16
The level of benefit paid	17
The cost to local government	19
Landlords benefit	21
3: The human cost	24
Slum conditions	24
Increased stress	26
The 'job trap'	27
The 'furniture trap'	28
Who suffers most	29
4: Stop the waste	31
The wrong approach	31
Improving conditions	32
Building more costs less	33
Comparative costs at the national level	34
Where the money comes from	36
Comparative costs for London	37
The costs in two London boroughs	38
The government could save money	38
More jobs	40
More investment makes sense	41
5: A more efficient solution	42
Notes	46
Appendix I: The new proposals on board and lodging payments	49
Appendix II: Proposed measures to be included in an HMO Bill	54

Acknowledgements

We should like to thank our colleagues at SHAC for their advice and assistance in the preparation of this report. We are also grateful to Nick Beacock, Chris Holmes, Jonathan Stearn, Matthew Warburton and Christian Wolmar for commenting on earlier drafts; to Ann Cross for her insight and time, and to several London boroughs for providing us with helpful information.

Introduction

The problem

Bed and breakfast accommodation is fast becoming a new form of slum housing in Britain. As the homelessness crisis worsens, an increasing number of households are having to rely on unsatisfactory bed and breakfast accommodation in order to secure a roof over their heads. For such people, this type of accommodation is normally overcrowded, usually in poor condition, and often insanitary. It is impossible to live a normal life in bed and breakfast establishments, nor can they be said to offer a 'home'. What they do offer is a roof over the heads of people who would otherwise be homeless, but at great public expense and human cost.

At the same time as the number of homeless people living in bed and breakfast accommodation has been increasing, public investment in housebuilding has been severely cut. Public expenditure on housing has been reduced by 55 per cent in real terms since 1979–80, and local authority house building is now at one of its lowest levels since the early 1920s. In addition, the government has reduced yet further the amount that local authorities can spend of the receipts they obtain from selling their own dwellings.

The people living in bed and breakfast accommodation as their 'home' fall into two main groups. First, there are those households, mostly families with children, who have been placed there by local authorities under the Housing (Homeless Persons) Act. Although bed and breakfast is meant to provide temporary accommodation for such people, the increasing scale of the homelessness problem has meant that 'temporary' usually means months and sometimes years. The number of households placed in bed and breakfast under the Homeless Persons Act in England has increased from 1,800 at the end of June 1979 to 3,020 at the end of June 1984. Second, there are other households who have found their own way into bed and breakfast accommodation. The vast majority are single people and childless couples who, together with some families, do not qualify for rehousing under the Homeless Persons Act.

The number of employed households living in bed and breakfast is not known; but the number of people on supplementary benefit classed as 'boarders' has risen from 49,000 in 1979 to an estimated 139,000 in 1984, an increase of 184 per cent in five years. Of these, only a small proportion (two to three per cent) are those placed in bed and breakfast by local authorities. The vast majority of boarders are not the responsibility of any local authority under the Homeless

Persons Act and have received relatively little attention from policy makers. It is very important, therefore, that discussion of bed and breakfast should not be confined just to those placed there by local authorities, for that is only a quantitatively small (albeit important) part of the overall problem. Accordingly, this report takes the wider view and considers the bed and breakfast problem as a whole.

Structure of the report

This report examines both the human and the financial cost of the marked increase in the number of people living in bed and breakfast accommodation. It also shows that a substantial increase in public sector housing to rent could provide a more effective and more economical way of dealing with the growing homelessness crisis.

Chapter 1 looks at why the number of people in bed and breakfast has increased so markedly. It shows that current government housing policy has itself been an important factor. It concludes that there is an urgent need for more investment in public sector housing to rent.

Chapter 2 outlines the enormous financial cost, to both central and local government, of relying on bed and breakfast as a form of accommodation. It shows that this expense, while currently necessary because of the shortage of housing to rent, only benefits the proprietors of bed and breakfast, many of whom have learnt to exploit the system.

Chapter 3 documents the human cost of bed and breakfast. The slum condition of many establishments causes a high degree of stress and is often a serious danger to the health and safety of residents.

Chapter 4 shows that there is a better way of dealing with the growing bed and breakfast crisis. The government's response has been to introduce proposals to restrict claimants' benefit. The chapter shows why that is the wrong way to tackle the problem and outlines a more efficient and economical solution. The report is able to demonstrate that it is actually cheaper to build more permanent homes to rent than to keep people in bed and breakfast. At the same time this would create much-needed employment in the construction industry. Finally, this report presents a package of proposals for dealing with the current crisis. A public sector new building programme is vital and urgent. It is also crucial that better standards are enforced in bed and breakfast establishments, to ensure that for as long as people do live there, they are in accommodation that is of a reasonable standard, and safe. The proposals make sound economic sense and would bring enormous social benefit.

1: Why the increase?

The increasing use of bed and breakfast hotels is directly related to central government housing policies. These policies have reduced the amount of housing to rent, while doing little to increase the total number of homes. As permanent housing becomes harder to find, particularly for those without a job, more people are finding that bed and breakfast is the only housing option open to them.

Cuts in public rented housing

Local authority capital spending has been severely reduced since the mid 1970s and in real terms has nearly halved in the last six years alone. This is largely the result of cuts in the capital allocation from central government to local authorities. In real terms, for every £100 allocated in 1977-78 only £32 is allocated in 1985-86. The 1985-86 allocation is £259 million less than in 1984-85, a cut of 19 per cent in real terms in one year alone.

As a result of these cuts, local authority new building programmes have collapsed and 130,000 fewer new homes to rent were started in 1984 compared with annual building in the mid 1970s in Britain, a drop of over 75 per cent. Local authority housebuilding is now at one of its lowest peacetime levels since the early 1920s. (Private building has not increased sufficiently to compensate for the fall in public building, and rarely caters for those who need to rent.) Public building programmes are continuing to decline, and Diagram 2 shows the forecasts of the Building Material Producers for the next few years.

In addition to the collapse of new building programmes to rent, councils have been encouraged to sell off their rented housing into owner occupation. Over 650,000 council homes have been sold since 1979.[1] About 30,000 of these were vacant and would otherwise have been immediately available to new tenants, while the rest were occupied but would have contributed vacancies in the longer term.[2]

With fewer new homes to let and losses from sales, local authorities are increasingly restricted in their ability to rehouse people from the waiting list or homeless families. They are also in

Diagram 1: Housing capital allocations and spending on new house building, England (£ million at 1985-86 estimated outturn prices).

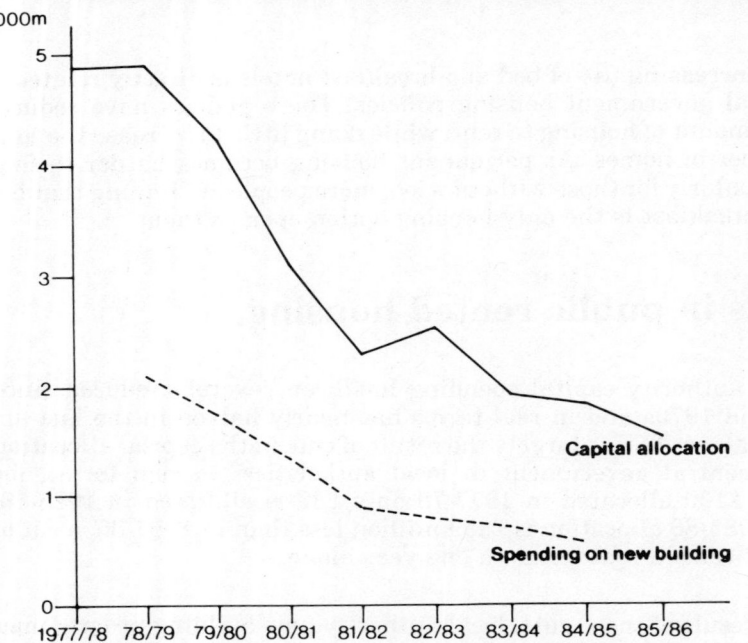

Sources: Capital allocations: London Boroughs Association, based on government figures.

Spending on new building: Based on The Government's Expenditure Plans 1984-85–1986-87, Vol. 2 Cmnd 9143-11.

many cases unable to provide the type and size of homes needed by new tenants. It is sometimes alleged that more use could be made of empty property, but a recent study by the Department of the Environment found that "long-term empty dwellings were almost entirely those which were undergoing or awaiting major physical work, sale or demolition. The single most important reason for these high levels of long term empties is the poor or defective condition of the stock, frequently compounded by problems of systems-built blocks and houses".[3] Many local authorities have been able to reduce the number of empty dwellings by better management practices and, while some authorities may still be inefficient in their use of the stock, the Department of the Environment found that mismanagement and procrastination were the exception, not the rule. Several authorities included in the study stated that the situation was made worse by "a lack of capital resources and an inability to plan long-term strategies because of the financial uncertainties inherent in the year to year allocation procedures."[4]

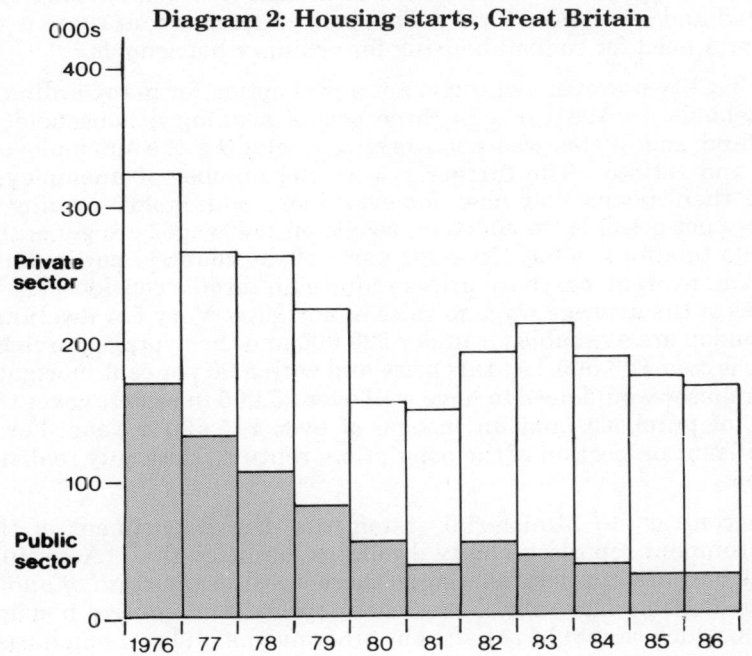

Diagram 2: Housing starts, Great Britain

Sources: 1976-83 Housing and Construction Statistics, Department of the Environment.
1984-86 Building Material Producers' forecasts.

The cuts in capital allocations to local authorities have seriously curtailed their ability to rehouse people off the waiting list, particularly in London where only 17,000 were rehoused in 1982–83 compared with over 30,000 a year for several years in the 1970s.[5] For those trying to find somewhere to rent, particularly those setting up home for the first time, the chances of getting a council home are shrinking, particularly in certain parts of the country.

The focus on owner occupation

The overriding concern of current government housing policy is to promote owner occupation. In a speech concerning new building activity, Patrick Jenkin, Secretary of State for the Environment, said "The Government regards this shift in balance from public to private sector in the provision of housing as highly desirable. It is our aim to sustain it as far as we can, subject to other social and economic objectives. But of course, we cannot look to the market to satisfy all needs. For a minority, new building by local authorities or housing associations is still essential though the task is today of a limited and specialised kind".[6] This policy assumes that there is no longer a need for council housing for ordinary households.

In reality however owning is not a real option for many ordinary households. In 1981, one in three people heading a household in England and Wales was not working, including the unemployed, sick and retired.[7] The further rise in the number of unemployed since then means that now, for even more households, owning is simply not possible. In addition, people on low wages are generally unable to afford to buy. In some parts of the country, particularly London, average purchase prices require an income considerably in excess of the average wage to raise a mortgage. Very few dwellings in London are available for under £20,000 and the average purchase price is over £43,500.[8] At this price and with a 90 per cent mortgage a purchaser would need to have well over £5,000 in cash to cover the costs of purchase, and an income of over £15,600 a year. For a significant proportion of the population, renting is the only realistic option.

In contrast to Ministerial statements, the Department of the Environment report on empty dwellings admitted that, "According to the best assumptions available, there is still *a short-fall of public sector dwellings* for rent to meet both special and general housing needs, which cannot be satisfied by other means".[9] (Their emphasis.)

The continuing shortage

It is also important to recognise that the increase in ownership promoted by current government policies has been achieved at the direct expense of renting, through existing rented properties (both public and private) being transferred into owner occupation. There has not been an adequate increase in the amount of private new building to compensate for the fall in public sector building and forecasts for the future, shown in Diagram 2, suggest a further decline. There is still a considerable shortage of housing. The Association of Metropolitan Authorities estimates the shortage to be over half a million dwellings; this is a low estimate because it assumes that more empty properties will be brought into use and it ignores the demand for separate accommodation from people living in bed and breakfast accommodation. Shelter estimates the shortage to be as high as 800,000 nationally.[10] Policies which change the tenure of properties but do not increase the amount of housing available do little to ensure that everyone who needs a home has one.

The continuing decline of the private rented sector

For those households that are unable to obtain local authority housing or who cannot afford to become owner occupiers, the alternative is accommodation rented privately. But the privately rented sector has been continuously declining in size for the past 70 years, as Diagram 3 shows, and now accounts for only a small proportion of the total housing stock. Every year the supply of privately rented accommodation gets smaller. The General Household Survey showed that, by 1983, the percentage of households renting their accommodation privately (excluding housing association tenants and those occupying accommodation rented with a business) had shrunk to only seven per cent of the total (see Table 1). The decline has continued since then and is almost certain to continue inexorably.

Diagram 3: Proportion of all dwellings rented privately, England and Wales.

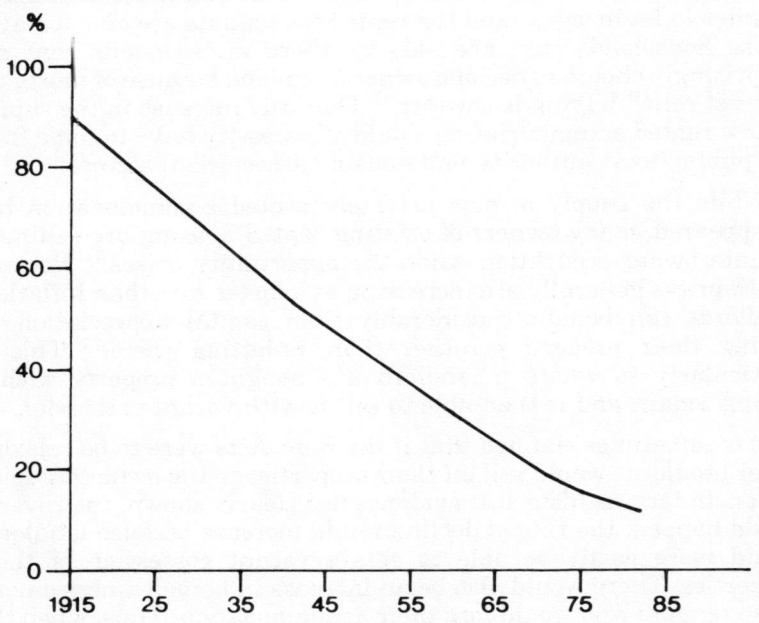

Notes:
a. Includes rented from private owners and other tenures, excluding owner occupied and public rented dwellings.
Source:
DoE Housing and Construction statistics.

Table 1: Percentage of all households renting privately 1973-83, Great Britain

	1973	1975	1977	1979	1981	1983
Rented privately, unfurnished	11	10	8	8	6	5
Rented privately, furnished	3	3	3	3	2	2
Total	14	13	11	11	8	7

Source:
OPCS Monitor, GHS 84/1, July 1984, p.6

This decline of the privately rented sector has been the result of a complex of social and economic developments and is a phenomenon common to countries in Western Europe and North America.[11] In Britain there has been virtually no new building in the sector at all since 1939. As the failure of the 'shorthold' and 'assured tenancy' schemes has emphasised, investment in privately rented accommodation is no longer an attractive proposition. The fundamental factor, as the House of Commons Environment Committee report on the sector recently pointed out, is that there is a large gap between the return on investment that investors *require* in order to let housing, and the rents that tenants are *able* to pay.[12] Those households that are able to afford an economic rent not surprisingly choose to become owner occupiers: because of mortgage interest relief, buying is cheaper.[13] Thus any increase in the supply of new rented accommodation would of necessity have to come from the public (local authority and housing association) sector.

While the supply of new privately rented accommodation has disappeared, many owners of existing rented housing are selling it off into owner occupation when the opportunity arises.[14] Because house prices generally are increasing at a faster rate than inflation, landlords can benefit considerably from capital appreciation by selling their properties rather than re-letting them.[15] This is particularly so where a landlord has bought a property with a sitting tenant and is then able to sell it with vacant possession.

It is sometimes claimed that if the Rent Acts were to be relaxed, fewer landlords would sell off their properties to the owner occupied sector. In fact, as historical evidence has clearly shown, the reverse would happen: the rate of decline would increase because landlords would more easily be able to obtain vacant possession of their properties. There would also be an increase in homelessness among those tenants who would lose their accommodation. Thus, when the Rent Acts were relaxed in 1923 and 1957, the rate of decline of the sector increased.[16,17] In both instances, Acts were subsequently introduced to protect tenants from eviction (The Prevention of Eviction Act 1924 and the Protection from Eviction Act 1964).

This increasing shortage of rented accommodation is particularly serious for those who are unemployed or are otherwise on a low income. Many landlords refuse to accept unemployed people as tenants,[18] while the costs of entry into the privately rented sector are increasingly prohibitive. For example, preliminary results from a SHAC survey currently being undertaken indicate that the average *minimum* rent for a one-bedroom flat now being quoted by accommodation agencies in London is £60 a week.[19] Most prospective tenants would be required to pay one month's rent in advance, one month's deposit and, if an agency is used to find the accommodation, two weeks' rent in fees to the agency—a total initial payment of £600 just to secure the accommodation.

The inevitable consequence

Thus households who cannot buy often cannot obtain rented accommodation either. Alongside the continuing decline of the privately rented sector, publicly rented housing has been subject to severe cutbacks. Yet there is a continuing need for rented accommodation for both families and for single people.

It is estimated that less than a fifth of the nine million single adults in England and Wales have been able to establish an independent home of their own.[20] In particular, censuses show that the number and proportion of people aged between 16 and 29 in Britain is increasing and is likely to continue to increase for some time. These are the newly-forming households who would be looking for independent accommodation for the first time. Advice agencies are finding that the majority of young people they assist have left their parental home as a result of overcrowded conditions or serious family tensions, or have not had a parental home at all.[21] They tend initially to move in with friends or relatives and will only move into board and lodgings as a last resort when other options fail. The Government's own research shows that the overwhelming majority of homeless single people want ordinary independent housing and few would choose to live in a hostel or bed and breakfast hotel.[22]

However, government policies are making it harder for many people to find independent, permanent housing, and for increasing numbers there is no option but to live in bed and breakfast accommodation.

2: The financial cost

The numbers increase

The increase in the number of households having to live in bed and breakfast accommodation has considerable cost implications, both for central government and for local authorities. Not only has DHSS expenditure on board and lodging payments increased, but also many local authorities place households, whom they have accepted under the Homeless Persons Act, in bed and breakfast accommodation prior to rehousing them.

While the growing shortage of rented housing is forcing both employed and unemployed households into bed and breakfast accommodation, the problem is particularly acute for the latter group of households. DHSS statistics show that the number of supplementary benefit recipients who are living in what it terms

Diagram 4: Supplementary benefit claimants in ordinary board and lodging accommodation, Great Britain, 1979–84

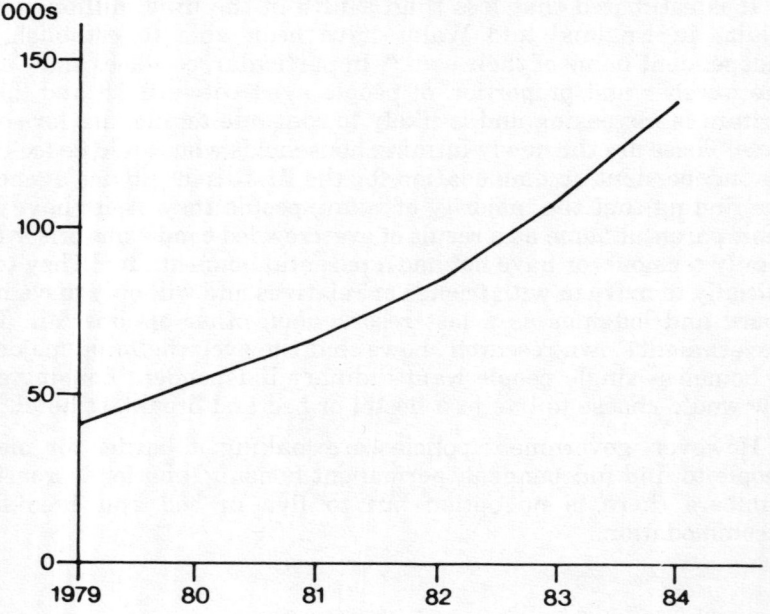

Source:
DHSS *Supplementary Benefit Board and Lodging Payments*, 1984

'ordinary board and lodging accommodation' has increased quite dramatically (see Diagram 4). Whereas in 1979 49,000 supplementary benefit recipients were living in board and lodging accommodation, by 1984 the number had increased to an estimated 139,000; an increase of 184 per cent in just five years.

These figures include recipients paying an amount for accommodation which includes cooked meals as well as those living in a hostel, guest house or hotel. Table 2 suggests that the increase in board and lodging recipients has occurred particularly among supplementary benefit recipients living in hotels and guest houses rather than those living in hostels and common lodging houses.

Table 2: supplementary benefit recipients receiving board and lodging allowances by type of accommodation, 1979–83, Great Britain.

Year	Hostels and common lodging houses	Other types of board and lodging
1979	24,000	25,000
1980	24,000	31,000
1981	31,000	38,000
1982	31,000	54,000
1983[a]	35,000	75,000
Increase:	11,000 (46%)	50,000 (200%)

Notes:
a. Provisional

Source:
Hansard, 14.11.84, cols. 661–662

Only a very small proportion (two or three per cent) of households living in bed and breakfast accommodation were placed there by local authorities; the vast majority of boarders are people who are not provided with assistance under the Homeless Persons Act. Indeed, most of the supplementary benefit recipients who are living in board and lodging accommodation are single claimants. For example, DHSS statistics for 1982 show that 97 per cent of all such claimants were single and only three per cent were couples (see Table 3).

Table 3: Couples and single people claiming supplementary benefit in board and lodging accommodation, Great Britain, 1982

	Boarders	Hostels & common lodging houses	Total No	%
Single people	52 252	29 797	82 049	97.3
Couples	1 369	902	2 271	2.7
All claimants	**53 621**	**30 699**	**84 320**	**100**

Source:
DHSS, *Annual Statistical Enquiry*, 1982

Table 4 shows the age distribution of supplementary benefit recipients claiming as boarders in December 1982 and in December 1983. In absolute terms, the increase in the number of such claimants was greatest among those aged 26 years or more. This age group accounted for 44 per cent of the 25,000 increase in claimants over this one year period. However, as Table 2 indicates, there has been a disproportionate increase in boarders aged under 26 years, especially those aged 21 to 25 years. These are people who in the past would often have been able to get work and establish their first independent household in the rented sector. But unemployment has increased by more than two million since 1979, and young adults have been particularly affected. For example, between July 1979 and July 1984, unemployment among young adults aged 18–19 increased by 156 per cent, and among those aged 20–24 it increased by 192 per cent.[23] Hence the twin pressures of very high rates of youth unemployment in recent years and the decreasing availability of rented accommodation have left many young people with little alternative (other than the streets) to bed and breakfast accommodation.

Table 4: Age distribution of supplementary benefit recipients claiming as boarders.

Age	1982[a] No.	1983[a] No.	Increase No.	%
16–17	4,300	6,700	2,400	56
18–20	8,500	13,300	4,800	57
21–25	10,400	17,200	6,800	65
26+	61,200	72,300	11,100	18
Total	**84,400**	**109,500**	**25,100**	**30**

Notes:
a. December figures
Source:
Hansard, 20.11.84, cols.119–20

The cost to central government

Just as the number of supplementary benefit recipients living in bed and breakfast accommodation has increased, so too has the cost of benefit paid. This is shown in Table 5. In outturn prices, the annual cost has increased from £52 million in 1979 to £380 million in 1984. In real terms, this is an increase (in 1982–3 prices) of 377 per cent in just five years.[24] Much of this increase in cost can be accounted for by the 184 per cent increase in claimants over the same period. However, as Table 5 indicates, there has been an increase in the average payment made, in outturn prices, from £20.40 in 1979 to £52.35 in 1984. In real terms, this is an increase of 67 per cent.

Table 5: Supplementary benefit board and lodging payments: the number of recipients, annual cost and average payment, 1979–84.

Year	Recipients	Annual cost[a]	Average payment
1979	49,000[d]	£52 m	£20.40
1980	55,000	£76 m	£26.60
1981	69,000	£115 m	£32.15
1982	85,000	£166 m	£37.80
1983[b]	108,000	£277 m	£48.05
1984[c]	139,000	£380 m	£52.35

Notes:
a. Based on December figures
b. Provisional
c. Estimate
d. The source for this table puts the figure at 41,000, but it is clear from *DHSS Statistics* and *Hansard* 14.11.84 that this is an error.
Source:
DHSS, *Supplementary Benefit Board and Lodging Payments*, 1984

The level of benefit paid

It would be wrong to assume, because there has been a real increase in the average amount of benefit paid to boarders on supplementary benefit, that claimants are any better off. This becomes apparent from an examination of what 'average payment' means and of how the amount of benefit boarders receive is determined.

The average payment made is a net figure, after taking into account any other income that claimants have, for example, unemployment benefit, child benefit and retirement pension.[25] Thus, if the average amount of non-supplementary benefit income that claimants have falls in real terms, other things being equal, the amount of supplementary benefit paid will in real terms increase. At least in London, as Table 6 shows, two thirds of boarders are unemployed claimants. With the growth in unemployment and also the abolition of Earnings Related Supplement, there has been a proportionate increase in the number of unemployed claimants solely reliant on supplementary benefit and a decrease among those solely reliant upon unemployment benefit.[26] Thus, to some extent the real increase in the average amount of supplementary benefit paid to those living in ordinary board and lodging is simply the result of an increased dependence of unemployed people on supplementary benefit.

Table 6: Boarders on supplementary benefit in the Greater London Area, 1982

	No.	%
Over pension age	2,500	15.9
Unemployed under 25	3,300	21.0
Unemployed over 25	7,400	47.1
All other allowance cases	2,500	15.9
Total	**15,700**	**100.0**

Source:
Hansard, 12.12.84, col.533

Supplementary benefit paid to claimants living in board and lodging accommodation includes an amount for 'personal expenses' and an amount to cover the bed and breakfast charge plus other meals. The amount for personal expenses is meant to cover day-to-day living expenses other than meals and lodging costs. The amounts paid for personal expenses are fixed sums per person depending upon the age of the members of the household. (For adults not required to register for work who have been on benefit for more than a year there is a slightly higher rate of benefit than for others.) The basic rate paid for personal expenses for an adult is currently £9.25 a week (i.e. only £1.32 a day). It is uprated each year by the increase in retail prices excluding housing costs.

The board and lodging part of the benefit covers the cost of lodgings plus meals up to a local maximum, known as the board and lodging 'ceiling'. If the charge that a boarder on supplementary benefit has to pay is above the 'ceiling', then the extra has to be met out of the allowance for personal expenses or by cutting back on meals. Housing advisers at SHAC find that it is often difficult to obtain accommodation for their clients that is within the 'ceiling'. For example, in one recent (December 1984) SHAC case, the adviser had to phone 51 'hotels' before it was possible to obtain somewhere for the family to stay. (This family were homeless but were not accepted for housing by the local authority under the Homeless Persons Act.) For unemployed claimants who have not contacted an advice agency like SHAC it would be financially impossible to phone this number of hotels.

Although the amounts quoted as being paid to supplementary benefit recipients living in bed and breakfast may seem substantial, the amount they receive for their day-to-day living expenses is small. The largest part of the payment is for the lodging charge, the ultimate beneficiary of which is the bed and breakfast proprietor.

The cost to local government

Some bed and breakfast residents have been placed there by local authorities because they are homeless. Local authorities will generally assist homeless families who fall within one of the priority groups identified in the Housing (Homeless Persons) Act 1977, that is:
- people with children or pregnant women;
- the elderly;
- people with a serious mental or physical problem or who are vulnerable in some way;
- people made homeless by an emergency such as fire or flood.

Not everyone who falls within these groups is eligible for council housing. Authorities are not obliged to rehouse people who have some form of housing to return to, and those who became homeless through their own actions (called 'intentional homelessness'). The number of homeless accepted for rehousing has risen steadily, from 34,000 in 1975 to an estimated 83,000 in 1984 (see Diagram 5).

Homeless applicants whose cases are being investigated sometimes have to be provided with temporary housing, and those declared intentionally homeless must be given temporary accommodation for a limited period. In addition, as the number of homeless households has risen and local authorities have had increasing difficulty finding suitable lettings, more homeless families who have been accepted are also having to be placed in temporary accommodation while waiting for a permanent home. Authorities have been trying to use a number of forms of temporary accommodation including hostels, short life properties and leasing privately rented housing; but it has not been possible to find enough such short-term housing. The use of bed and breakfast accommodation has fluctuated over the last few years but there has recently been a marked increase.

Table 7: Local authority homeless households in bed and breakfast on June 30th, England

Year	Number
1978	1,230
1979	1,800
1980	2,050
1981	1,620
1982	2,030
1983	2,460
1984	3,020

Source:
Department of the Environment homelessness statistics

Diagram 5: Homeless households accepted by local authorities, England.

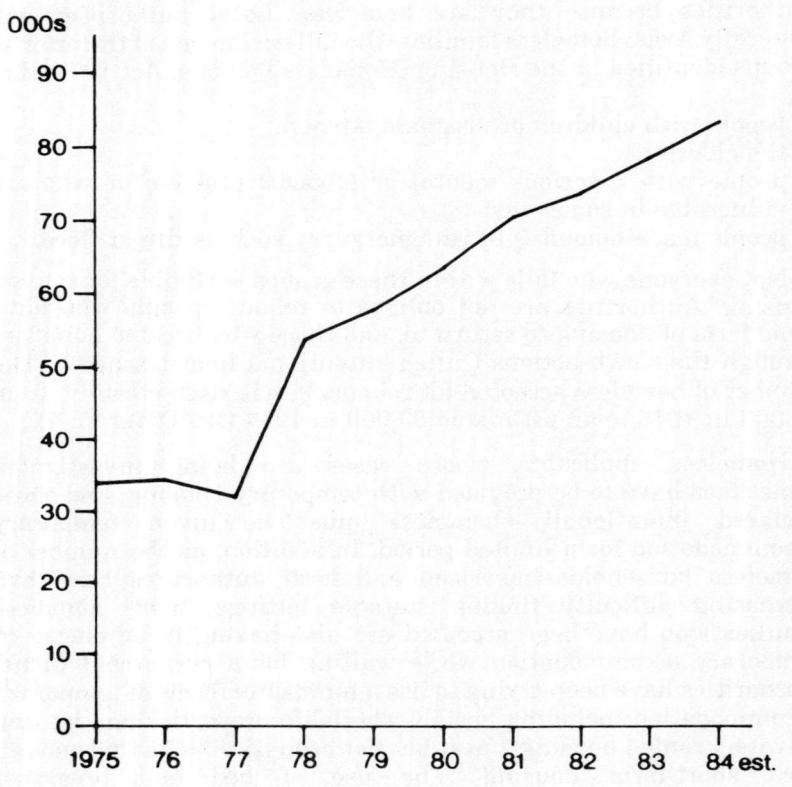

Source:
DoE homeless statistics. The Housing (Homeless Persons) Act was introduced at the end of 1977. The basis for recording statistics changed at this date.

The increase has been especially marked in London with over 2,000 families placed in bed and breakfast in June 1984. Almost 80 per cent of London boroughs make use of bed and breakfast accommodation; the only boroughs who never do so are all in outer London.[27] However, the use of so-called 'hotels' has increased in all areas, not just in the major cities.

The acute shortage of suitable council housing has also meant that in some areas people are having to stay in bed and breakfast accommodation for long periods of time; months and in some instances years. In June 1984 the London Borough of Brent predicted that "families being accepted as homeless now are likely to average at least three years in temporary accommodation".[28] Since then the numbers placed in temporary accommodation by Brent have increased and the average waiting time is also likely to have lengthened. This cannot be called 'temporary accommodation'.

Keeping homeless families in bed and breakfast hotels is very expensive for local authorities. For example if a hotel charges £40 per person per week, a family with two children would cost well over £8,000 a year. Local authorities get some of the money back from the families' own incomes or DHSS support, but this often falls short of the total hotel bill which the local authority has to pay. The total net cost to local authorities in England and Wales in 1983–84 is estimated to be well over £10 million, and is half as much again as in the previous year.[29]

This cost to local authority budgets must be added to the cost to the DHSS of board and lodging payments, to see the total cost to the public purse of such a great and increasing use of bed and breakfast accommodation. In addition to these immediate, measurable costs, there are wider social costs resulting from extended bed and breakfast living, especially for families. These include increased use of health services and greater demands on education services for children.

Landlords benefit

This enormous public cost benefits no one except the owners of bed and breakfast establishments. While most genuine hotels continue to cater exclusively for visitors, some provide residential accommodation during the off-season winter months, while others do not cater for the holiday trade at all but rent rooms entirely to people wanting somewhere to live. There is no public control on charges and the Rent Acts do not cover this type of accommodation. Hotel owners can therefore charge what the market will bear, and some owners have learnt to exploit the system.

Within the group of hotels providing residential accommodation, some specialise even further and accommodate only homeless families placed there by local authorities. A major advantage in catering for this group is that in general the local authority will pay the bill and recoup the money from the family, thus providing guaranteed payment which the hotel owner does not have to chase up. Some of these owners in particular seem to be exploiting the situation to make considerable profits. The DHSS ceiling for bed and breakfast payments (excluding lunch and dinner payments) is currently fixed by the local DHSS offices, and ranges from about £20 a week in some parts of the country to £98 in the most expensive parts of central London. Some so-called 'hotel' owners price their rooms close to the local DHSS ceiling. At the national average DHSS limit for bed and breakfast of about £50 a week per person, a medium sized hotel with five single, five double and five triple rooms, could bring in about £1,500 a week. In the most expensive parts of London such a property could give an income of nearly £3,000 a week if prices were set at the local DHSS board and lodgings ceiling.

The greatest use of hotels for homeless families accepted by local authorities occurs in London. With at least 18 boroughs searching for bed and breakfast accommodation for their homeless families, often outside the borough boundaries, hotel owners are able to bid up their prices even above the local DHSS ceiling. A recent report by the London Borough of Haringey states that many hotels charge a much higher price to homeless families accepted by the borough than to other residents.[30] Owners are also able to charge more to those boroughs who have greater numbers of homeless families to accommodate, and the same hotel may charge different rates to different boroughs. One West London hotel charges one borough £28 a week per person more than it charges another.[31]

In addition, it appears that some hotel owners operate together, and knowledge of how much a borough is prepared to pay at any one time quickly spreads to a number of owners who raise their prices accordingly. Local authorities thus find themselves having to pay more as the pressure from homeless families increases.

By exploiting the system in this way, some owners are able to generate considerable income from their properties. It is estimated that one hotel in central London with 150 beds is taking in £700,000 a year; this hotel is used by homeless families from at least three London boroughs.[32]

There are therefore substantial financial incentives for some property owners to shift from providing holiday accommodation to providing residential accommodation for DHSS claimants, and in some areas even more income can be made by catering specifically for local authority homeless families. There is evidence that some property owners are converting what was previously privately rented accommodation into such hotels because the potential profits are so much greater. For example, there is currently a legal dispute over a property in North Kensington where the residents dispute the owner's claim that it is now a hotel. The property has no external signs showing it to be a hotel and, in claiming their rights as tenants of a privately rented property, the residents allege that they have had to partially furnish their rooms and pay for their own heating.[33]

Because of the acute shortage of housing, particularly rented housing, there is a demand for bed and breakfast accommodation which property owners are able to exploit. They benefit at huge public cost.

3: The human cost

Slum conditions

As a way of tackling the housing shortage, bed and breakfast accommodation is expensive not only in financial terms but also in human terms. Although such accommodation does at least provide a roof over a household's head, it can hardly be said to provide a 'home'. Moreover, the condition of much bed and breakfast accommodation is very often appalling. In effect, the state is subsidising a new form of slum housing as a result of its failure to ensure a sufficient supply of rented accommodation.

Bed and breakfast accommodation includes not just lodging houses and hostels but, increasingly, hotels. For many people, the word 'hotel' conjures up an image of comfort or even luxury. However, while some of the bed and breakfast hotels being used to house people who would otherwise be literally homeless do have an air of respectability from the outside, inside they are often dingy, damp, overcrowded, insanitary fire traps. The same is true of many other types of 'houses in multiple occupation'.

Although the standards and facilities provided in bed and breakfast accommodation vary, they are in many cases seriously deficient. Many establishments are in a poor state of repair. Amenities are often lacking or seriously inadequate. For example, a SHAC study of families that had been accepted for rehousing by local authorities found that, of the households that were placed in bed and breakfast hotels, 89 per cent had just one room for their exclusive use, 94 per cent shared a bathroom and 95 per cent shared a toilet.[34] Single people often have to share a room with strangers.[35]

Overcrowding is also common. For example, one family visited by SHAC are, at the time of writing, living in one room in a five-storey hotel in Bayswater. The family consist of a husband and wife plus their four small children. Taking up almost the entire floor space are two double beds placed side by side; the bedding is minimal and dirty. There is virtually no other furniture in the room: there is not enough space. Approximately two feet from the beds, located behind a sliding door, is a toilet, wash basin and bath, cramped together. There are approximately 150 other rooms in the hotel, many of them housing homeless families and single people. The lift in the hotel is not working. The stairs are narrow and steep. In another hotel a family, also visited by SHAC, consisting of a couple with a four month old baby, is living in a small basement room with a low ceiling. The baby sleeps in the pram because there is no room for a cot. The family has been living there since August 1983.

Many hotels are also dangerous fire traps, lacking adequate fire escapes, fire doors and extinguishers.[36] The Olympus Hotel fire, in which a mother and her two children died, is a recent example of just how inadequate fire precautions sometimes are in hotels and other types of houses in multiple occupation (HMOs). According to press reports, an employee of the hotel, who raised the alarm, tried six fire extinguishers, all of which were found to be empty. Escape routes from the five storey hotel were blocked and there were said to be no fire escapes or balconies.[37] Fire investigators found that as many as seven people were sleeping to a room.[38]

The facilities provided in many bed and breakfast establishments are very poor indeed. Some do not have hot water, while in others it is only available at certain times of the day. Some rooms do not have water at all. Lack of (hot) water is a particularly serious problem for the parents of young babies, for without suitable washing facilities it is difficult to keep clean or sterilise bottles and other feeding utensils.[39] Facilities for the washing of clothes are also commonly inadequate or non-existent. Again, this is a particularly serious problem for the parents of children who are still in nappies. Launderettes may be located some distance from hotels and are expensive. Not surprisingly, although it is often in contravention of hotel rules to do so, residents often resort to washing clothes in their room or shared bathroom.[40]

Heating is also a problem in some hotels. Residents do not always have control over the level of heat or the period for which it is provided. Hence room temperatures can be either too hot when the heating is on or too cold when it is off.[41] In other hotels, the heating is simply inadequate all the time, a problem that is of most concern where there are young babies.

Cooking facilities are almost invariably inadequate or non-existent in bed and breakfast establishments. While some hotels do provide a communal kitchen, these are often very dirty, badly maintained and not very accessible for many residents.[42] A kitchen located in the basement is not much use to people who live on, say, the fourth floor of a hotel, many flights of stairs and several corridors away. In this situation a parent may have to face the choice of leaving the children unattended in the room, with all its hazards, while they cook, or of taking them to a crowded, dirty, perhaps dangerous kitchen.

Not surprisingly, many residents choose not to use the kitchen even where one is provided.[43] Instead, they either buy ready made food at a cafe or 'take away', or attempt to cook in their rooms on temporary hot rings—the latter often located on the floor in the space between bed and wall and therefore within reach of small children and babies. The risk of burns or even of fire, in these circumstances is considerable. Because of the generally inadequate cooking facilities for the residents of bed and breakfast establishments it is difficult to maintain a proper balanced diet. Intestinal disorders are common and health visitors in the Paddington area have even found cases of malnutrition.[44]

Many residents experience several or all of these problems at the same time and thus suffer from their cumulative effects. This can be illustrated by reference to a SHAC client, Mrs G. Along with her five children and two grandchildren, she lives in two small rooms in a guest house in Bayswater, London. The charge for the two rooms, according to Mrs G., totals £300 a week. There are no cooking facilities. Both hot water and heating are available only for three hours in the morning and three hours in the evening. Despite problems with bed bugs they have to sit in bed for much of the day in order to keep warm. The children suffer from stomach problems and the family as a whole from general ill health. According to their doctor, the youngest child has scabies. They have been living in the guest house for nearly a year.

Increased stress

Lack of play space for the children is a difficult problem facing families living in bed and breakfast accommodation. The cramped conditions common in bed and breakfast establishments make play very difficult, especially for older children. With the hazards of, for example, fires and cooking rings, parents have constantly to be on the alert lest their children come to harm within their room. In many cases, hotel managements insist that children be confined to their room all day and do not play in corridors or on stairs.[45] This creates stress both for the children and their parents whose task it is to keep them confined. As one separated single parent living in one room in a bed and breakfast hotel reported:

> "Well, being restricted, it's keeping them back, because if they had a home they could go in other rooms, but you have to keep shouting at them and they get frightened of you. So it means staying in one room has affected them."[46]

In the SHAC survey, 54 per cent of families in bed and breakfast hotels reported changes in their children's behaviour that were solely for the worse; only four per cent reported changes for the better. Yet among families who had been placed in permanent accommodation, a much smaller percentage (32 per cent) reported changes for the worse, while 31 per cent reported changes for the better.[47]

The stresses and strains of living in bed and breakfast accommodation can often have a detrimental effect upon the relationship between couples. In extreme cases, it can even lead to violence and relationship breakdown. In the SHAC survey, 28 per cent of the couples interviewed shortly after they had been placed in bed and breakfast by the local authority admitted that their relationship had changed for the worse. Yet when the families were interviewed a year later, when many of them were no longer living in bed and breakfast accommodation, many couples said that their relationship had improved.[48] For example, Mr and Mrs P had by then moved to a permanent home from their temporary accommodation:

> "We were very irritable with each other and there were terrible strains—we couldn't even make love. We had more rows. Everything's been fine since we moved home though."[49]

Indeed, the SHAC survey found that both relationship problems among couples and the behavioural problems of children often improved considerably once the family had been moved into permanent accommodation.

In general, bed and breakfast accommodation is of a low standard with limited facilities and, often, serious fire risks; there are immense social restrictions and very limited privacy. It is, however, impossible to quantify, or even adequately to convey in words, the squalid, depressing, debilitating life facing the residents of such accommodation. While bed and breakfast hotels may provide a roof over the heads of people who have nowhere else to stay, they certainly cannot be said to provide a 'home' in any real sense of the word.

The 'job trap'

For unemployed people not accepted for rehousing by their local authority, there is the further problem that, if they are fortunate enough to be offered a job, they may not be able to afford to continue to live in bed and breakfast accommodation. Although people in work may be eligible for housing benefit, this will usually cover only a part of the accommodation element in the bed and breakfast charge.[50] At the same time, their supplementary benefit will of course cease, and their pay may not be sufficient to make up the difference. Such people may therefore be faced with the dilemma of having to choose between taking the job and possibly losing what accommodation they have, or refusing the job; a cruel choice to have to make when jobs are so difficult to obtain. If people in these circumstances were living in permanent accommodation, this sort of situation would be unlikely to arise.

The 'furniture trap'

One of the absurdities of the present homelessness problem is that, even where supplementary benefit claimants are fortunate enough to be offered unfurnished accommodation, many are being refused furniture grants by the DHSS.[51] As a result, the would-be tenant has either to refuse the offer of accommodation or take the flat and sleep on the floor, with no cooker or furniture.

The DHSS justify such refusals on the grounds that there is 'suitable alternative furnished accommodation available in the area'.[52] It is up to claimants to prove that there is no such suitable accommodation at all. Bed and breakfast accommodation is regarded by the DHSS as a 'suitable alternative' form of furnished accommodation.[53] Yet all the evidence shows that this is *not* a suitable form of permanent accommodation. For a claimant to be offered the tenancy of a local authority or housing association flat, she or he must either have been on a waiting list for a number of years or be judged a special case deserving immediate rehousing. Moreover, the offer of a flat means more than just accommodation: it represents security of tenure and often the ending of years of waiting and of hardship. The frequent refusal by the DHSS to give furniture grants illustrates a complete lack of understanding of the housing market.[54] It is a classic example of the failure of separate government departments to achieve a joint approach to social policy.

The refusal of a furniture grant can actually cost the state more over a period of time than the award of one if, as a result, the claimant gives up the offer of a tenancy and moves back into bed and breakfast accommodation.[55] Rents for unfurnished accommodation are generally much lower than for furnished accommodation. The cost over time to the DHSS (in housing benefit plus a furniture grant) of maintaining a claimant in unfurnished rented housing will, in general, be considerably less than the cost of maintaining a claimant in expensive bed and breakfast accommodation.

The 'suitable alternative furnished accommodation' clause should be abolished. Instead, the test of eligibility for a single payment for furniture should be that of need. This would not only simplify administration and be fairer for claimants, it could also save money.

Who suffers most

The appalling conditions in much board and lodging accommodation affect all types of residents, but certain types of people are more likely to live in this type of accommodation and for longer periods, while others may experience the problems associated with living in board and lodgings more acutely. Where a resource such as housing is in short supply, what housing there is will not necessarily go to those in greatest need, or to those who experience a range of disadvantages in society, for example single people with special needs, black and Asian households, and households headed by women.

The majority of board and lodgings residents are single people. Single people have generally not been catered for by local authority allocation policies, and the shrinking of the privately rented sector has particularly affected the single who have traditionally relied on such accommodation. In addition, the closure of many institutional hostels, particularly in London, has further reduced their housing options. The number of single people, particularly the young, without a home has increased sharply over the last few years.

Some single people have special needs for some form of social support. Among the priority homeless groups which local authorities will accept are those people regarded as vulnerable through disability, handicap, old age or some other reason. In this way, some single people with special needs do become the responsibility of local authorities. It is estimated that in 1984 over 6,600 vulnerable homeless people were accepted by local authorities, excluding the elderly.[56] However, in many cases single vulnerable people accepted by the local authority are then placed in bed and breakfast accommodation for considerable periods of time, which is wholly unsuited to their physical and social needs. In additon many people with special needs are not accepted by local authorities at all because they do not apply or are not considered 'vulnerable'; such people may also find themselves living in bed and breakfast through a lack of alternatives. For example, SHAC recently helped a single registered disabled woman who had been rejected as vulnerable by an inner London borough. She moved into bed and breakfast accommodation because there was no alternative, and within a week was admitted to a psychiatric hospital with a nervous breakdown. The borough has now accepted her under the Homeless Persons Act, but has placed her in bed and breakfast accommodation until permanent housing becomes available.

The opportunity to create a normal lifestyle and compensate for other disadvantages is much reduced when the basic resource of housing is so unsatisfactory. People need to be coping extremely well with all aspects of their lives in order to be able to handle some of the conditions which prevail in bed and breakfast accommodation, and those with special needs are often not in this position.[57] The pressure of demand from this group is increasing as the Government's 'Care in the Community' policy is having the effect of discharging more people from psychiatric hospitals and other institutions without adequate provision for their rehousing. Unless there is a major programme to provide suitable permanent housing, there will be increasing numbers of people with physical and social problems trying to cope in the most difficult housing conditions.

A number of studies have shown that black households are disproportionately represented amongst the homeless accepted by local authorities, and are therefore more likely to be placed in bed and breakfast accommodation.[58] In addition, in some areas Asian households are disproportionately represented among the very large households, and the acute shortage of large council dwellings means that Asian households are trapped in bed and breakfast accommodation for particularly long periods of time. The recent pressures from homeless families in the London Borough of Camden have highlighted the particular problems that large Bengali families are facing.

Women experience housing problems acutely because of their weak economic position, because they tend to spend more time in the home than men, more often have the care of children, and are vulnerable to violence in the home. Therefore women are likely to be particularly affected by the problems of coping with living in bed and breakfast accommodation with children, where conditions are cramped, there is a high level of sharing, a lack of privacy and of facilities. Children are brought up with restricted lives where there is no space to play, and noise levels are a constant source of conflict and tension.

Most bed and breakfast residents are simply people who cannot find anywhere else to live but those who are disadvantaged in other ways are particularly vulnerable to the poor conditions, and are more likely to be trapped there.

4: Stop the waste

It is clear that this policy by default, of relying on bed and breakfast accommodation to make up for the shortage of permanent rented housing, is neither economic, efficient, nor effective. A far better solution would be to increase the supply of housing available to rent within the means of those in need, so that fewer people would have to live in bed and breakfast accommodation.

The wrong approach

Unfortunately, the Government's response to the increasing use of bed and breakfast accommodation has been to penalise the victims rather than address the causes of the problem. The DHSS has recently put forward proposals to restrict the circumstances in which, and the period of time for which, recipients of supplementary benefit can claim as boarders.[59] A new, 'normal local office area' restriction is to be introduced. It is also proposed permanently to replace the existing locally-determined board and lodging limits with two, centrally-determined limits (one for Greater London, one for elsewhere); the limits which are proposed are unrealistically low and it is not intended to increase them until November 1986.

If implemented, the proposed changes would have very serious consequences indeed for a large number of people who currently have no choice but to live in bed and breakfast accommodation. They would result in a considerable increase both in people who have literally nowhere to stay, and in overcrowding in grossly inadequate accommodation for those who are lucky enough to find anywhere in their 'normal local office area' within the new limits. The ability of unemployed boarders to move in order to seek work will also be severely restricted.

Not only are the DHSS proposals ill-considered, they are also based on a number of assumptions which bear little relation to the nature of the problem of homelessness. The consultation document which contains the proposals displays neither an analysis of, nor any apparent concern for, the likely consequences for claimants of the proposed changes, something that is extraordinay for a department that is responsible for social security and income maintenance. (The proposals are discussed in more detail in Appendix I.)

These proposals illustrate a serious lack of inter-departmental liaison between the DHSS and the DOE. In simply aiming to cut expenditure, the DHSS is acting in isolation. No account seems to have been taken of the extent to which the growth in board and lodging expenditure since 1979 has been a consequence of cuts by the DOE in capital investment over the same period. This directly parallels the cuts made during 1984 by the DHSS in housing benefit levels. The cuts were introduced to stem the growth of housing benefit expenditure. Yet a major reason for this increase was the sharp withdrawal in general subsidy to local authority housing revenue accounts made by the DOE in order to increase rents, as a result of which more people were eligible for housing benefit. (Indeed, the fall in general subsidy more than offset the rise in housing benefit expenditure.)[60] It is clear that there is an urgent need at central government level for the 'joint approach' to social policy called for as long ago as 1975 by the Morris Committee on Housing and Social Work.[61]

Improving conditions

Instead of penalising claimants by cutting benefit, the government should introduce a positive programme for tackling the bed and breakfast problem. In addition to a substantial increase in investment in public house building, there is an urgent need for immediate action to improve conditions within bed and breakfast establishments and other types of Houses in Multiple Occupation (HMOs) in order to ensure the health and safety of residents. Such action should include the introduction both of a system of registration of bed and breakfast establishments, and of an act governing standards and conditions in HMOs.

A system of registration of bed and breakfast establishments should be introduced in order to prevent abuse by proprietors. Under such a system, the rates that proprietors could charge would be set locally and would vary according to the standard of accommodation offered. Proprietors would thereby have an incentive to improve conditions in their establishment, while board and lodging charges could be kept under control. By contrast, the government's proposals on board and lodging, if implemented, would result in a lowering of standards and more overcrowding. A system of registration along these lines already operates successfully in many European countries and there seems to be no reason why such a system could not also be introduced in Britain.

The administrative machinery to operate a registration system already exists in the Rent Officer service. It is not proposed that the 'fair rent' system be applied to the bed and breakfast sector, but rather that the expertise of rent officers be used. This would establish a viable system that prevents abuse but allows establishments to charge an economic rate for the accommodation they provide. Establishments could be divided into broad categories on the basis of the standard of accommodation and facilities provided. Within each of these broad categories, a maximum charge per room/person could be determined. (To prevent overcrowding, there would need to be a limit to the number of people that could be resident in any particular room in an establishment.) These rent bands could be increased annually in line with an agreed index such as the retail price index. Such a system would provide an incentive for proprietors to improve conditions within their establishment in order to move into the next rent category, while profiteering would be prevented.

In addition, the Houses in Multiple Occupation Bill, which passed its second reading in the last Parliament with the support of 100 MPs but fell with the general election, should be enacted. Its provisions include setting national minimum standards for houses in multiple occupation, and requiring local authorities to inspect and enforce these standards. More details of the proposals are given in Appendix II.[62] The measures proposed would both strengthen and simplify the current complex array of legislation. If enacted, they would benefit not only residents in bed and breakfast establishments and other HMOs, but also local authorities who currently have difficulty implementing the present legislation. Even more, if enacted and carried out, these measures would save lives.

Building more costs less

It is possible to estimate the total cost of building additional council dwellings and contrast this with the costs of keeping people in bed and breakfast accommodation. The relative costs are first considered here for the country as a whole using national average figures. They are then presented for London using London average figures, and finally the actual cost comparisons in two London boroughs are examined.

Looking first at the cost of building an extra council dwelling, Department of the Environment Housing and Construction figures suggest that the average cost of a new local authority, two storey, four bedspace house in 1984 was approximately £23,400 including land and fees. This would be suitable for a family with one or two children. Recent tender prices in London suggest that a one bedroomed dwelling suitable for a single person or a couple costs about £2,000 less than a two bedroomed four person dwelling.[63] Local authorities normally borrow the money to build from the money market, and repay the loan with interest over 60 years. The annual debt charge on a loan of £23,400 at a rate of interest of 10 per cent would be approximately £2,350, and on a loan of £21,400 would be around £2,150.[64] In real terms, this cost reduces over time due to inflation. This fall in the real costs of debt charges is considerable: for example with inflation at a steady 5 per cent the real cost in the tenth year would be only 63 per cent of the cost in the first year. These figures show the marginal cost of building one extra council dwelling.

The annual cost of providing one council dwelling is the debt charges on the loan plus the running costs. The management costs for normal local authority housing are approximately £100 per dwelling per year.[65] Repair costs are likely to be minimal in the first year of a new dwelling but will increase in later years. However, this is almost certain to be offset by the reduction in the real costs of debt charges over time. (At national level in 1983–4 the running costs for council housing including all management and repairs amounted to less than 60 per cent of the gross rent income, the remainder of which was available to pay debt charges on previous investment.)[66]

Comparative costs at the national level

It is now possible to contrast the total public cost of keeping a household in board and lodgings with the cost of rehousing the same household in a new council home. The following calculation assumes the household has no income but is receiving supplementary benefit. The amount of supplementary benefit is different for a household living in local authority accommodation (known as a 'householder') and for the same household living in bed and breakfast accommodation (known as a 'boarder'), to reflect the difference in living expenses in each type of accommodation. Therefore supplementary benefit has been included on both sides of the balance sheet to give a true, complete comparison. The rates vary depending on the household type, so three different types of household are presented. The board and lodgings payment is made on a per person basis and therefore increases sharply with increasing household size. However, owners of bed and breakfast accommodation also generally charge on a per person basis, and the DHSS payment would immediately be passed on to the owner as rent.

A supplementary benefit recipient can claim housing benefit to cover the full cost of the rent. This has the effect of transferring the money from one part of the public purse to another, but is not an additional cost. The rent contribution and housing benefit costs have therefore not been included in the costs of providing council accommodation presented below.

Couple with two children (one under 11, one under 16)

Board and lodgings:	£ per year
DHSS full board and lodging payment[1]	11,075
DHSS personal expenses allowance[2]	1,374
Total cost in board and lodgings	**12,449**
Council accommodation:	
Debt charges	2,350
Management	100
DHSS supplementary benefit[2,3]	3,624
Total cost in council accommodation	**6,074**

Couple no children

Board and lodgings:	
DHSS full board and lodging payment[1]	6,882
DHSS personal expenses allowance[2]	965
Total cost in board and lodgings	**7,847**
Council accommodation:	
Debt charges	2,150
Management	100
DHSS supplementary benefit[2]	2,375
Total cost in council accommodation	**4,625**

Single person

Board and lodgings:	
DHSS full board and lodging payment[1]	3,441
DHSS personal expenses allowance[2]	482
Total cost in board and lodgings	**3,923**
Council accommodation:	
Debt charges	2,150
Management	100
DHSS supplementary benefit[2]	1,463
Total cost in council accommodation	**3,713**

Notes:

1. The average local limit for full board and lodgings in December 1983 was £66 a week per adult. Since then there have been considerable increases in some local limits, while on the other hand the average payment will be less than the limit. In the absence of any information on the effects of these two factors, the £66 a week figure has been used. This includes an allowance for

meals of up to £1.55 daily for lunch and the same for dinner. The maximum full board and lodgings payment for children under 11 years is £14.40 a week.
2. This is calculated at the ordinary scale rate and assumes the household has no special needs in respect of diet, laundry etc.
3. This does not include the heating addition of £2.10 a week paid in respect of children aged under 5.

The above illustrations, and the calculation for any type of household, show a clear financial benefit in providing council accommodation rather than maintaining people in bed and breakfast accommodation. This is in spite of the fact that the assumptions used give unfavourable figures for council provision. The figures given show the first year costs of council building; as the real costs of debt charges will reduce year by year, while the costs of board and lodgings are likely to rise over time, the balance will become increasingly favourable for council provision.

There are a number of additional factors which would further strengthen the advantage of council provision, although they are difficult to measure. The wider social costs of extended bed and breakfast living, resulting in greater use of social, health and educational services are, for example, ultimately a public cost resulting from inadequate housing. It is also important to stress that while board and lodging payments are a drain on public funds for no return, local authority building provides a long-term public asset which will benefit several generations.

Where the money comes from

The figures given above show the maximum possible costs to the public purse of providing council accommodation against maintaining a household in board and lodgings. These costs can be met from a number of different sources. Board and lodging accommodation costs are entirely met by central government through the DHSS; for local authority homeless families there may be additional topping-up costs to the local authority.

The costs of council accommodation are paid out of the local authority Housing Revenue Account, and the income may come from four main sources: council rents, interest on the sale of property and land, a government subsidy, and a subsidy from the local rates. Local authorities operate a rent pooling system whereby the rents on older property, with low or no debt charges, help to subsidise the rents on new property with higher debt charges. In this way, the rents from the existing stock help to underwrite the costs of additions to the stock. Sales have been providing an increasing income to local authorities over the last few years and may give some authorities the scope to provide new accommodation to make up the loss of properties sold. The government subsidy to authorities' Housing Revenue Accounts is worked out by a formula which links together the costs of running council accommodation and the rents. The subsidy is calculated individually for each local authority in the country and the level is different in each area. In an increasing number of areas the formula results in no government subsidy being payable at all: three quarters of authorities in England are not receiving a subsidy in 1984–5. Similarly, in many local authorities there is no subsidy from the rates to the Housing Revenue Account, but instead the Account has a surplus which is used to subsidise the rates; the picture varies greatly from one area to another.

Comparative costs for London

The calculations shown above are based on national averages. London is the most expensive part of the country in which to provide council accommodation. The local DHSS ceilings for full board and lodgings vary greatly within London, from under £70 to nearly £120 a week. The calculations for London have therefore been worked out for two different levels—£80 a week and £100 a week. Using London-wide figures for the price of construction and land,[67] and management expenses,[68] the relative costs are estimated as follows:

£ per year	Board and lodgings	Council accommodation
Couple with 2 children	14,638/17,767	7,601
Couple	9,307/11,393	6,152
Single person	4,653/5,696	5,240

Even in London there is still a significant financial advantage in providing council accommodation for most household types. For single people however the balance is more evenly drawn and depends more critically on the local level of DHSS board and lodging payment. However, in areas where this payment is lower, the cost of building council accommodation may also be lower than the London average. It is also important to bear in mind that the figures show the first year costs only; within a few years there is likely to be a considerable financial advantage for council provision for all household types. The unquantifiable costs mentioned above would have the effect of further increasing the relative advantage of council provision.

The costs in two London boroughs

Two boroughs, one in inner London and one in outer London, have been selected to show the actual comparative costs in specific areas. The costs of council building are taken from the PCI forms, which boroughs submit to the Department of the Environment for building approval; these include construction costs, a market valuation of the land, and all fees. The average general management costs for each borough are used. For bed and breakfast costs, the local DHSS ceilings are used. In the case of homeless households placed in bed and breakfast by the boroughs, the actual costs may sometimes be greater than the local ceiling where the boroughs are forced to use more expensive accommodation.

In the inner borough, there are few large sites for development and most council house building is taking place on small infill sites which tend to be expensive to develop. A scheme of one bedroom flats approved by the DOE in 1984 costs £45,400 per dwelling. No two bedroom four person houses were built in 1984 but the DOE formula for approving schemes would allow a maximum cost of about £60,000 for such a dwelling. These costs are used in the calculation. The borough includes part of Central London with very high local DHSS bed and breakfast ceilings (£98 excluding meals), and the costs for bed and breakfast have been worked out both for this ceiling, and also for the lower ceiling of £90.30 excluding meals which applies in most of the rest of the borough.

The outer borough has considerably lower local DHSS ceilings for bed and breakfast (£64.70). The cost of council building is also much lower than in inner London, with one bedroom flats costing £35,106 in one recent scheme and two bedroom dwellings costing £43,665.

	Board and lodging £ per year	Council accommodation £ per year
Inner borough		
Couple with 2 children	20,848/19,644	9,817
Couple	13,447/12,644	7,107
Single person	6,723/6,322	6,195
Outer borough		
Couple with 2 children	15,640	8,083
Couple	9,975	5,977
Single person	4,987	5,065

The example shows that in the inner borough it is cheaper to provide new council accommodation, for all types of household, than to maintain people in bed and breakfast accommodation; the savings for families are very considerable. In the outer borough it is cheaper to build for couples and families, but for single people it may cost slightly more. In the example used this cost is £78 in the first year, and with reducing real debt charges in later years it is unlikely that there would be much, if any, additional cost in subsequent years.

The government could save money

While the figures used are tentative and have been based on a number of assumptions and averages, the scale of the differences between the costs of maintaining people in board and lodgings and providing new council accommodation are so great in most cases that the financial benefit of council provision is undeniable. In addition there are substantial social benefits in providing permanent housing. In other words, the government could save money by encouraging more council homes to be built. An expanded building programme would bring immediate and lasting financial advantage to the public purse, as well as enormous social benefit.

Some local authorities have tried to make the same point to the government in different ways in relation to their own use of bed and breakfast for homeless families. The London Borough of Camden has calculated that it would cost less to rehabilitate its own properties for short life use than it is costing to keep families in bed and breakfast hotels. For example, a four bedroomed house, which would accommodate a family of seven people, would cost £32,000 to rehabilitate for a five year life, whereas the council is actually paying £10,470 a year to keep such a family in bed and breakfast, which would amount to over £52,000 over the five years.[69] Yet the Department of the Environment has refused the majority of the borough's applications to spend money rehabilitating such larger dwellings to suit the needs of homeless families. Some years ago another London borough sought government permission to purchase a private hotel to use as cheaper temporary accommodation for the homeless; this proposal was also rejected. By restricting the expansion of the public sector the government is perpetuating the financial waste of such a high use of bed and breakfast accommodation.

More jobs

The above balance sheet shows the immediate financial advantage of increasing council housing provision. However, there are other long-term benefits, which are also significant in their financial as well as their social impact; building creates jobs.

To illustrate this point, it is possible to estimate the number of jobs which would be created by £100 million worth of new house building work, and the consequent Exchequer savings as unemployment is reduced. It has been estimate elsewhere that each £1,000 worth of contract creates about 13 days of work for an on-site operative.[70] £100 million would therefore create about 1.3 million days of work, or about 5,500 person years. It has been found that for every three on-site jobs in the construction industry, there is one off-site professional or clerical worker, so the total extra jobs created in the construction industry would be of the order of 7,400.[71] Additionally, increased levels of investment have multiplier effects in the building supply and transport industries, and an even wider effect as the extra income is spent. While these wider effects are difficult to measure, it has been estimated that for every extra job in the construction industry, one additional job is created in the wider economy.[72] This means that the original £100 million building investment could have the effect of providing work equivalent to nearly 15,000 jobs a year.

This additional employment would bring savings to the Exchequer in unemployment and supplementary benefits and would bring extra income through taxes. There are indications that the cost per unemployed person in overall public expenditure terms is at least £5,000 a year.[73] Therefore, on the basis of the above assumptions, the saving made by £100 million building programme in creating the equivalent of 15,000 jobs could be of the order of £74 million.

This calculation is of necessity tentative, built on assumptions based on the best available information. However it does clearly illustrate that investment in building brings considerable financial as well as social benefits.

These findings are entirely in line with a growing number of economic studies which have shown that increased public investment is by far the most effective measure which the government could take to reduce unemployment and boost the economy. For example, a recent comparison of the relative benefits of tax cuts and public investment, using the computer models of the economy of the London Business School, the National Institute of

Economic and Social Research and the Treasury itself, clearly favoured public investment.[74] This was so even when the effect of these two alternative options on interest rates was taken into account. These tests showed that, after two years, public investment would reduce the dole queues by between two and four times as much as tax cuts.

More investment makes sense

A number of recent studies have indicated that there is a desperate need for increased investment in Britain. For example, an international comparison recently carried out by the Organisation for Economic Co-operation and Development showed that investment in Britain is amongst the lowest in the industrial world, and it is particularly low in construction.[75] Residential construction as a percentage of GDP is much lower in Britain than in every other EEC country and has fallen from 3.8 per cent in 1976 to 2.1 per cent in 1981, a decline of 45 per cent in five years.[76] Thus, increased investment in public sector house building would go some way towards bringing residential construction in Britain nearer to a level that is comparable with that of other industrial nations.

The government has cut back housing investment on the grounds that it is essential to reduce public borrowing. Increased investment in public sector house building could be funded in two ways, each of which would have a different effect upon public borrowing: local authorities could either borrow the money or be allowed to spend a much higher proportion, if not all, of their receipts from council house sales. If local authorities used their current year capital receipts, this would not increase public borrowing and would neither help increase interest rates nor add to the money supply.[77] If some of the money necessary to fund a house building programme were obtained by borrowing, this would by definition add to the Public Sector Borrowing Requirement. However, in recent years the Local Authority Borrowing Requirement has been very small and in 1982 was negative.[78] The definition of the PSBR does not distinguish between capital and current spending; in reducing the number of people in bed and breakfast, increased local authority house building would allow a shift from current to capital expenditure.

These investment arguments for increased house building can be added to the evidence presented earlier in this paper that building new homes could actually reduce the day to day outlay from the public purse. Increased housing investment makes sound economic sense and would reduce the massive human suffering of those who have nowhere to live but bed and breakfast accommodation.

5: A more efficient solution

This report has looked at the rapidly growing problem of bed and breakfast accommodation. Its increased use is the result of government policies which have restricted the rented sector while failing to increase the total number of homes. With a large unmet need for independent permanent housing, many people are left with no option but to live in bed and breakfast.

As the number of supplementary benefit claimants in board and lodgings has increased the cost to central government has soared. At the same time, local authorities are having to pay increasing amounts to support more homeless families in bed and breakfast establishments, and for longer periods of time.

Conditions in many bed and breakfast 'hotels' are appalling and dangerous. The stress of living in such conditions is having wider social costs which are difficult to quantify.

The Government's response to this problem has been to introduce proposals penalising those who cannot obtain decent housing, by cutting DHSS benefit payments. SHAC argues that this would significantly increase hardship and homelessness while not tackling the fundamental problem of insufficient suitable housing. The Government had done nothing to reduce the number of homeless families placed in bed and breakfast by local authorities.

What is needed is a package of action to tackle the problem at a number of levels.

1. Building homes to rent

It has been shown in this report that the public outlay required to build more council homes to rent would, in most circumstances, be less than the outlay required to keep people in bed and breakfast accommodation. In addition such a building programme would create jobs and bring further substantial savings to the Exchequer. The fear that such investment, by increasing the Public Sector Borrowing Requirement, would be to the detriment of the wider economy, is unfounded.

It would take a few years for local authorities, housing associations and the building industry to gear up to an increased level of activity. Therefore, the need to begin expanding the programme is urgent if the growing housing crisis is to be halted.

- The Government should immediately increase the local authority and Housing Corporation capital allocations, and make a

commitment to continue to do so each year until investment is at least twice the current level.
- The Government should allow local authorities to spend all of their capital receipts with no time restrictions.
- Local authorities should immediately plan to increase the provision of rented accommodation both in the local authority and housing association sectors.
- Local authorities should review their policies, particularly towards single people, to remove arbitrary barriers which restrict access.

2. Better standards

Even if the use of board and lodging accommodation were to be reduced, action should be taken immediately to protect the residents, as well as those living in other forms of houses in multiple occupation.
- The Government should establish a mandatory system of registration of bed and breakfast establishments including control of standards and rent levels.
- The Government should enact a Houses in Multiple Occupation Bill to ensure better standards (as outlined in Appendix II).
- Local authorities should inspect all bed and breakfast establishments regularly and enforce the existing legislative standards.

3. Reduction in bed and breakfast use by local authorities

Local authorities must be encouraged to make major efforts to eliminate the use of bed and breakfast accommodation, except in extreme circumstances.
- The Government should enforce the Housing (Homeless Persons) Act 1977 Code of Guidance which says that bed and breakfast accommodation should only be used for very short periods of time and only in exceptional circumstances, and local authorities should immediately adhere to the Code of Guidance in these respects.[79]
- Local authorities should make further efforts to reduce the number of empty properties to a minimum.
- Authorities should vigorously pursue all possible alternative types of short-term housing including hostels, short life use of

their own property and joint schemes with housing associations and with the private sector.

- Authorities should not place vulnerable people in bed and breakfast hotels.

- Authorities should plan their housing provision so that it meets the requirements of the homeless, particularly those with large families.

4. More realistic board and lodgings payments

Many organisations and agencies, including SHAC, have strongly urged the Government not to go ahead with proposed changes to the system for providing board and lodgings payments. Appendix I explains this in detail.

- The Government should immediately withdraw the proposed changes.

- The Government should allow local DHSS offices to set realistic board and lodgings payment limits.

- The Government should abolish the 'alternative furnished accommodation' restriction on the award of furniture grants to people moving from temporary to permanent housing, and ensure quick payment of these grants.

5. A co-ordinated approach to social policy

The current bed and breakfast crisis highlights the lack of co-ordination of social policies between different government departments, and the absence of consideration of the relationship between capital and current spending. The recent problems with the new housing benefit system showed the same lack of co-ordinated planning, with serious consequences for the claimants, those operating the system, and administrative costs.[80] The Government should learn from this experience.

- The Government should adopt a co-ordinated approach to social policy and consider together the housing stock and those who live in it.

- The Government should consider the relationship between capital and current spending and recognise that a reduction in the former may cause an increase in the latter.

The above recommendations present a package of action which is urgently needed if the bed and breakfast problem is to be tackled. The Government dismisses any argument for increased public investment in housing on the grounds that the money is not available. In a recent interview, Mr Ian Gow, Housing Minister, is reported to have said: "Anybody who has responsibility for housing recognises that there is a case, indeed there is a need, for more expenditure on housing. But we have to remember this. It isn't just a question of saying we want to have more money to spend. We have to conduct our financial affairs within the necessary constraints on public expenditure of all kinds. I am totally committed to the policy of sound money and honest finance."[81]

This report demonstrates that building more council homes is cheaper for the public purse than providing no alternative to bed and breakfast accommodation. SHAC argues that increased investment in rented housing is a policy of sound money and honest finance, which no Government can afford to ignore.

Notes

1. H.M. Treasury, *The Government's Expenditure Plans 1985–86 to 1987–88* (HMSO 1985).
2. Department of the Environment, *Housing and Construction Statistics* (HMSO, annual and quarterly).
3. Department of the Environment, *Local Authority Empty Dwellings* (DOE, January 1985), para.5.10.
4. *Ibid*, para.5.19.
5. S. Majasi, R. Matthews and T. Shotton, *Waiting Lists* (Shelter, 1984).
6. Patrick Jenkin, Secretary of State for the Environment, in a speech to the Housebuilders' Federation, Department of the Environment, *Press Notice*, 25.11.83.
7. Office of Population Censuses and Surveys, *Census 1981*.
8. Nationwide Building Society, *Quarterly Bulletin*, fourth quarter 1984; Halifax Building Society, *Quarterly Bulletin*, fourth quarter 1984.
9. DOE, *Empty Dwellings, op.cit.*, para.5.21. Their emphasis.
10. Association of Metropolitan Authorities, *Submission to the Inquiry into British Housing* (AMA, August 1984).
    Shelter, *The Housing Shortage*, Briefing paper 1983.
11. M. Harloe, 'Decline and fall of private renting', *CES Review* No.9, 1980, pp.30–34.
12. House of Commons, *First Report from the Environment Committee: The Private Rented Housing Sector*, (HMSO, 1982), Vol.1, p.XIii.
13. *Ibid*, Vol.2, written submission by SHAC, pp.91–99.
14. This point is discussed at length in S. Merrett, *Owner Occupation in Britain*, (Routledge & Kegan Paul, 1982) chapter 9.
15. J. Doling and M. Davies, *Public Control of Privately Rented Housing* (Gower, 1984).
16. P. Kemp, *The Transformation of the Urban Housing Market in Britain c.1885–1939*, (University of Sussex D.Phil. thesis, 1984), ch.12.
17. *Report of the Committee on the Rent Acts*, (HMSO, 1971), p.80; see also House of Commons, *op.cit.*, Vol.1, p.XXIV.
18. Central London Social Security Advisers Forum, *The Sort I'm Trying to Get Rid Of* (CLSSAF, 1984), p.8; London Borough of Haringey Comprehensive Housing Service, *Response to the New Board and Lodging Proposals of the DHSS: Social Security Advisory Committee Consultative Document (sic)* Issued 30 November 1984; see also note 19 below.
19. SHAC Accommodation Agency Survey December 1984/January 1985. 56 per cent of the accommodation agencies contacted by SHAC stated that they would not consider unemployed people.
20. Information obtained from CHAR (Campaign for Single Homeless People).
21. Threshold Centre, *Threshold Annual Report 1984* (Threshold, 1984).
22. M. Drake, M. O'Brien and T. Biebuyck, *Single and Homeless* (DOE/HMSO, March 1982).
23. S. Cusack and J. Roll, *Families Rent Apart* (CPAG/Youthaid, 1985), Table 2, p.3.

24. Converted from outturn to constant (1982/3) prices using the GDP deflator implied in H.M. Treasury, *The Government's Expenditure Plans 1984–85 to 1986–87*, (HMSO, 1984), Vol.1.
25. DHSS, *Supplementary Benefit Board and Lodging Payments: Proposals for Change* (DHSS, 1984), annex.
26. H.M. Treasury, 1985, *op.cit.*, Table 3.12.6 and para.14, p.172.
27. Greater London Council, *Temporary Accommodation—Long Term Problem* (GLC, January 1984), Ref.HG741.
28. London Borough of Brent, *Housing Committee Report*, 4.6.84, para.9.4.
29. Based on Chartered Institute of Public Finance and Accountancy, *Homelessness Statistics 1983/84 Actuals* (CIPFA, January 1985).
30. London Borough of Haringey *op. cit.*, p.7.
31. Information supplied by London borough housing officers.
32. *The Observer* 1.7.84.
33. *Kensington News and Post*, 28.9.84.
34. G. Randall, D. Francis and C. Brougham, *A Place for the Family: Homeless Families in London* (SHAC, 1982), p.19.
35. Threshold Centre, *op.cit.*, p.13.
36. A. Grosskurth, 'When home is a B&B hotel', *Roof* (Shelter, January/February 1984), p.12.
37. *The Standard*, 21.11.84; *London Housing* (SHAC/Roof, December 1984), p.4.
38. *The Standard*, 21.11.84.
39. Interview with Paddington health visitor, 31.1.85; Grosskurth, *op cit.*, pp.11–12.
40. Randall, *et.al., op.cit.*, p.19.
41. Grosskurth, *op.cit.*, p.14.
42. Interviews with hotel residents, 31.1.85; Randall, *et.al., op.cit.*, p.19.
43. In the SHAC survey half the families usually ate in cafes or restaurants and a fifth bought 'take away' meals to eat in their rooms. Randall, *et.al., op.cit.*, p.19.
44. Interview with Paddington health visitor, 31.1.85; Grosskurth, *op.cit.*, pp.12–13.
45. Grosskurth, *op.cit.*, p.13.
46. Quoted in Randall, *et.al. op.,cit.*, p.31.
47. *Ibid*, p.30.
48. *Ibid*, pp.29–30. Of the couples who said there had been a change in their relationship, 63 per cent said it had been for the better.
49. *Ibid*, p.30.
50. See CHAR, *Housing and Supplementary Benefits Guide 1985* (CHAR, 1984); P.McGurk and N.Raynsford, *A Guide to Housing Benefits* (SHAC, 1984).
51. Central London Social Security Advisors Forum, *op.cit*.
52. Single Payment Regulations (SI 1981 No.1528), Reg.10(1)(a).
53. CLSSAF, *op.cit.*, p.5.
54. *Ibid*, p.5.
55. CHAR, *Bare Boards: Guide to DHSS Furniture Grants* (CHAR, 1984), Chapter 7.
56. Department of the Environment, *Homelessness Statistics*.

57. Threshold Centre, *op.cit.*
58. For example, Commission for Racial Equality, *Housing in the London Borough of Hackney: Report of a Formal Investigation* (CRE, 1983).
59. DHSS, *op.cit.*
60. P. Kemp, *The Cost of Chaos: A Survey of the Housing Benefit Scheme* (SHAC, 1984), pp.62–73.
61. cf. Scottish Development Department, *Housing and Social Work: A Joint Approach* (HMSO, 1975).
62. See also *Taking Action to End Bedsit Squalor* (HMO Group, 1983).
63. Recent tender prices in the London Borough of Haringey.
64. At the time of writing, Minimum Lending Rate is 14 per cent, but is expected to fall. The 'real' rate of interest (i.e., Minimum Lending Rate minus the rate of inflation) is currently at an historically very high level.
65. Chartered Institute of Public Finance and Accountancy, *Housing Revenue Account Statistics*. Supervision and management, General; this excludes Special which covers the cost of wardens, lifts, etc.
66. *Ibid.*
67. DOE, *Housing and Construction Statistics* (HMSO).
68. CIPFA, *Housing Revenue Statistics, op.cit.*
69. *Inside Housing*, Vol.2, No.2, 11.1.85.
70. Shelter, *Build Homes, Build Hope* (Shelter, November 1981); AMA, *Building for Tomorrow: Housing Investment, Construction and Employment* (AMA, April 1982).
71. J. Stevenson, 'Go Forth and Multiply', Building (5.6.81), Vol.CCXL, No.7193.
72. Trades Union Congress, *The Reconstruction of Britain* (TUC, 1981).
73. AMA, *Building for Tomorrow, op.cit.*,
74. *The Guardian*, 3.1.85.
75. *Ibid*, 3.1.85 and 21.1.85.
76. *Hansard*, 20.7.84, col.312·
77. P.M. Jackson, *Local Authority Capital Expenditure Controls*, paper prepared for the AMA, p.19.
78. *Ibid*, p.16; Central Statistical Office, *Social Trends*, No.14, 1984 Edition (CSO, 1983), Table 6.19, p.96.
79. DOE, *Housing (Homeless Persons) Act 1977 Code of Guidance (England and Wales)*, Annex 2.
80. Kemp, *Cost of Chaos, op.cit.;* National Association of Citizens' Advice Bureaux, *Housing Benefit: The Cost to the Claimant* (NACAB, 1984).
81. *The Times*, 3.1.85.

Appendix I: the new proposals on board and lodging payments

In the consultation document *Supplementary Benefit Board and Lodging Payments* (November 1984) the Secretary of State for Social Services has put forward proposed amendments to the regulations governing board and lodging payments to recipients of supplementary benefit. If agreed by Parliament, the changes will come into effect at the end of March 1985. The main changes are:

(i) Responsibility for setting the maximum amounts of benefit payable to boarders will be transferred on a permanent basis from adjudication officers in DHSS local offices to the Secretary of State.

(ii) The existing, locally determined limits for ordinary board and lodging accommodation will be replaced by two new limits:
 a) £60–£70 pw in Greater London;
 b) £50–£60 pw elsewhere.

(iii) There will be restrictions on the eligibility of 16–17 year olds to claim board and lodging payments in their own right.

(iv) Most other unemployed people without dependants who claim outside what is deemed to be their 'normal local office area' will be awarded boarder status for only two to four weeks.

The DHSS had to submit these proposals, in accordance with section 10 of the Social Security Act 1980, to the Social Security Advisory Committee for its consideration. In turn, the SSAC invited interested bodies to submit to it their views on the proposals. SHAC is extremely concerned about the likely consequences of the proposed changes, should they be introduced, and we reprint below part of our submission to the SSAC.

Response by SHAC to the Social Security Advisory Committee on the DHSS Proposals on Board and Lodging Payments

1. Board and Lodging Limits

(i) The switch from locally determined board and lodging limits to centrally determined limits set by Ministers is a retrograde step. Locally determined limits can be set according to varying local circumstances, thus permitting a degree of fine tuning that is not possible in practice with limits set by Ministers. While it may be that there is at present a range of local limits that is not justified by variations in labour and housing market conditions, the proposed new system (of two limits, one for Greater London, another for outside London) virtually ignores the variations that are legitimate. The Consultation Document accepts that the system introduced in

November 1983 "still lacks precision", yet the proposed changes in respect of ordinary board and lodging accommodation will eliminate such precision as there already is and replace it with an inflexible set of limits (from which there will be no right of appeal) determined by Ministers in London.

(ii) We are also seriously concerned about the level of the new limits for ordinary board and lodging. It is clear from our extensive experience of helping homeless people in the Greater London area that the proposed limit of £60–£70 a week is quite inadequate. There is very little accommodation in London available at such a low level and what little there is is of the very poorest standard, much of it unfit for human habitation. The Consultation Document itself accepts that the limits will be too low in places such as central London with the result that "claimants will have to accept only basic standard accommodation or look in cheaper areas". How claimants on supplementary benefit are to find the means to look in cheaper areas is not explained but the suggestion is, in any case, directly contrary to the proposed new powers concerning claimants' normal local office area (which we discuss below). Similarly, to suggest that claimants will have to accept 'only basic shared accommodation' demonstrates an apparent lack of knowledge about conditions in board and lodging and 'hotel' accommodation. Often such accommodation is only very basic and sharing is common: the proposed changes would simply encourage even more overcrowding and force claimants to live in the most appalling accommodation. For families with children who have to rely on board and lodging accommodation but who cannot find anywhere within the proposed new limits, the result may be that their children have to be taken into care.

(iii) A far more effective method of dealing with abuse by proprietors—instead of the proposed changes which punish the victims—would be to introduce a system of registration. The rates that proprietors could charge would be set locally but would vary according to the standard of accommodation offered and they would therefore have an incentive to improve the conditions in their establishment. A system of registration along these lines already operates in many European countries and there seems to be no reason why such a system could not be introduced in Britain also. In contrast, the proposed changes are likely to result in a lowering of standards and more overcrowding.

2. Boarder Status

Even more worrying, however, are the proposed new powers to restrict the circumstances in which people may be paid as boarders and to limit the duration of such payments.

(a) 16–17 year olds claiming as boarders in their 'normal local office area':

(i) The proposal to restrict payments to 16 and 17 year olds claiming in their 'normal local office area' will result in hardship and increased homelessness for many people. The assumption behind the proposal is that such claimants have not only left home through choice but that they would be accepted back by their parents. Our own experience, however, suggests that this comfortable assumption is in many cases quite wrong. Young adults are sometimes forced to leave by their parents and will not be allowed to go back. In other cases, young adults have left because of severe overcrowding, violence or sexual abuse and would therefore be unwise to attempt to return to their parents' home even if they were allowed to. Many 16 and 17 year olds who can't go back to their parental home will therefore end up on the streets with no roof over their heads at all if these proposals are put into practice. A further assumption behind this proposal is that the parents of these young adults have themselves a home, but this is not always the case: in some instances, their parents are also homeless.

(ii) The Consultation Document states that 16–17 year olds "should be advised that they can, exceptionally, be paid as boarders if they fall within certain specific categories". This wording implies (it is not candidly stated one way or the other) that even people who are in these exceptional categories (e.g. young people who are pregnant or who have dependent children) will automatically be awarded non-householder status only. It will be quite possible, consequently, that such people may not be advised of their right to be assessed as a boarder and that it may in fact take weeks or even months (perhaps after an appeal in disputed cases) for them to be so assessed. In the meantime, they will have to live on the streets with consequent risk to their health and safety.

(b) Unemployed people without dependants claiming benefit outside their 'normal local office area':

(i) The proposal to limit payment to other unemployed people without dependants outside their 'normal local office area' to between two and four weeks in a particular locality is very disturbing and again reveals a lack of understanding of the problems facing people looking for work and more permanent accommodation. It also contradicts the Government's own advice to unemployed people to be prepared to move to find work rather than expect it to come to them.

(ii) The proposed new power assumes that the particular locality in which a claimant claims benefit as a boarder is entirely a matter of choice and that people should only be allowed to claim on other than a short-term basis, in what is deemed to be their 'normal local office area'. Unfortunately, the distribution of board and lodging accommodation is not even but rather concentrated in particular parts of cities. For example, there is very little board and lodging accommodation in Dagenham but a considerable concentration of it in Bayswater and Finsbury Park. In placing homeless families in board and lodging accommodation, London boroughs often have to use establishments in other boroughs because there is little available in their own area. Thus it will not always be possible for claimants to find accommodation within what is deemed to be their 'normal local office area'. Nor are jobs always available in a claimant's 'normal local office area', especially in localities where unemployment is at above average levels. Thus the proposal to place a time limit on benefit to boarders who are claiming outside their 'normal local office area' is both unfair and unrealistic.

(iii) Notwithstanding the folly of restricting the period for which claimants outside their 'normal local office area' can be assessed as boarders, the actual time limit that is proposed is completely unrealistic. With three million people unemployed and permanent accommodation very difficult to secure, few people could hope to find work and/or a home within only two to four weeks. What are claimants supposed to do when their two to four weeks have expired? If they cannot move back to what is deemed to be their 'normal local office area' their options will be either to sleep in the open or move on to another locality and claim there for a further two to four weeks and so on.

3. 'Normal Local Office Area'

(i) The proposed new powers on boarder status are based on the concept of claimants having a 'normal local office area', yet this term is nowhere defined in the Consultation Document. It is not at all clear what meaning this rather dubious concept will have in practice. It is one of the facts of modern life that people do not remain in one particular locality all their lives but move throughout the course of their lifecycle. The choice of which particular area is one's 'normal local office area' is therefore likely to be somewhat arbitrary, except perhaps in the case of single people who have just left home. The only non-arbitrary normal local office area that could be designated to many claimants would be that of their birth, as with the Elizabethan poor law.

(ii) The apparent reason for introducing this new regulation seems to be the belief, as expressed in the popular press, that young unemployed claimants are descending on seaside towns and enjoying a 'life style' not normally available to them. Yet no figures have been produced to show that a significant number of young people are moving to seaside towns. If the problem really is one of young people moving to seaside towns then there are ways of dealing with this without indiscriminately penalising all boarders outside their 'normal local office area'. The proposed new powers are effectively a sledgehammer being introduced to crack a nut.

4. Examples

Some typical examples of our clients who will be made homeless if the proposed changes are put into effect.

The first three cases are families for whom the local authority has refused to accept responsibility for rehousing under the Housing (Homeless Persons) Act. They are all living in the cheapest accommodation it was possible to obtain at the time.

1. *Mr & Mrs W.* Two children (aged 6 months & 18 months). They previously lived in tied accommodation in W12. After losing this

accommodation, they contacted SHAC. Our housing advisor had to ring 51 'hotels' before finally being able to place the family in a hotel in W2, the charge for which (£26 per night or £182 per week) is substantially in excess of the proposed new limits. If the new limits are put into effect, the family will be made homeless.

2. *Ms P.* Single parent with a son aged 8, living in one room in bed and breakfast accommodation in London. The room has a sink but no cooking facilities. The charge of £98 per week is above the proposed new limit. She will be made homeless if the proposed limits are put into effect.

3. *Ms C.* Single parent with two children (aged one and two). She is paying £105 per week for a hotel in SW5. If the new limits are put into effect, she will become homeless.

4. *Ms P.* Single woman, suffering from diabetes, previously living in private rented flat. Lost this accommodation having received poor advice from solicitor (now being sued for negligence) after landlord sought possession. Is now living in bed and breakfast, for which she is paying £63 per week and paying separately for her other meals. As the total is above the proposed new limits, she will become homeless if they are put into effect.

5. *Ms K.* Was previously living with friends outside London but was told to leave. Is now staying in a hostel in NW1, sharing a room. Under the proposed new powers about 'normal local office areas', she could be made homeless.

6. *Mr W.* Single man. Returned to Britain in November 1983 after an extended stay abroad. Since then has moved between Westminster and Kensington and Chelsea. The allocation of a 'normal local office area' will therefore be quite arbitrary.

7. *Ms J.* Was previously a joint tenant of accommodation in W10, but was forced to leave because of violence from her alcoholic partner. She is registered disabled. She is now living in a women's aid refuge and claiming at a new office. Under the proposed new powers about 'normal local office areas', she could be made homeless.

Appendix II: Proposed measures to be included in an HMO Bill

The introduction of a Houses in Multiple Occupation Act is essential in order to ensure improved conditions within bed and breakfast hotels as well as other types of HMO. The original HMO Bill, introduced by Jim Marshall MP, received a Second Reading in Parliament in February 1983. Unfortunately, the Bill lapsed with the June general election. The original Bill has since been revised by the HMO Group to take account of the views of the local authority associations and others who were consulted.

The six key provisions of the HMO Bill now are:

1. Anyone who owns or runs a HMO, including a bed and breakfast establishment, would be under a duty to ensure the health, safety and welfare of all occupiers.
2. National minimum standards would be set for amenities, space, management, fire precautions and means of escape in different types of HMO.
3. Local authorities would be required to inspect their areas for HMOs at least once every 2 years and keep an open record of their inspections and any action taken.
4. Local authorities would be required to enforce minimum standards and would have simple, speedy procedures for enforcement.
5. Local authorities would be obliged to close properties which could not meet required standards at reasonable cost, and would have a duty to rehouse in suitable alternative accommodation all those displaced.
6. If either the owner or the council failed to take action, occupiers would have the right to go to ocurt to get the conditions improved.

SHAC Publications

Research Reports

A Fair Hearing? Possession Hearings in the County Court (*April 1977*)	£3.25
Caught in the Housing Trap: Employees in Tied Housing (*October 1979*)	£1.20
Good Housekeeping: An Examination of Repair and Improvement Policy (*March 1981*)	£2.75
A Place for the Family: Homeless Families in London (*September 1982*)	£3.25
Working the Act: The Homeless Persons Act in Practice in Six London Boroughs (*September 1982*)	£3.50
What Price Housing? (*3rd edition, June 1984*)	£3.50
Housing Benefit: The Way Forward (*June 1984*)	£1.50
Capital Decay (*September 1984*)	£3.75
Cost of Chaos (October 1984)	£3.95

Rights Guides

A Guide to Housing Benefits	£4.50
Rights Guide for Home Owners	£2.50
Housing Rights Guide	£4.50

Housing Aid Booklets

Homeless? Know Your Rights	£0.40
Somewhere to Live in London	£0.50
Private Tenants: Protection from Eviction	£0.60
Your Rights to Repairs: A Guide for Council Tenants	£0.70
Your Rights to Repairs: A Guide for Private and Housing Association Tenants	£0.70
Your Guide to Housing Benefit:	
1. For Council Tenants	£0.60
2. For Private & Housing Association Tenants	£0.60
3. For Home Owners	£0.60
The Right Move: A Guide to Mobility and Housing	£0.50
Buying A Home	£1.00
Moving Home in Retirement	£0.85

Research Subscription Service

If you need to keep in touch with the latest developments in housing policy, you should join our research subscription service.

You will receive SHAC's latest report and the four subsequent reports over a period of approximately 18 months. The cost of a subscription is £14 for organisations and £11 for individuals and voluntary groups. Contact SHAC's Research Department for further details.